Puntastic Dad Jokes Book
Full of the Best Dad Puns out There

Father's Day Gifts

Dad, can you put the cat out?

I didn't realize it was on fire.

If prisoners could take
their own mugshots,
they'd be called
cellfies.

I got hit in the head with a can of Coke
today.

I'm fine though.

It was a soft drink

Do I enjoy making courthouse puns?

Guilty

At a restaurant
with Dad.

Hostess: Do you have reservations?

Dad: No. I'm confident I want to eat here.

A ham sandwich walks into a bar and asks
for a beer.

The bartender says, "Sorry, we don't serve
food here."

I was going to tell a joke about dogs but it seemed a little far-fetched.

I sold my vacuum cleaner, it was just gathering dust.

Not sure if you have noticed, but I love bad puns. That's just how eye roll.

When Dad buys milk.

Cashier: Would you like it in a bag?

Dad: No thanks, just leave it in the bottle.

The rotation of earth really makes my day.

My kid wants to make a pencil with an eraser on each end, but I just don't see the point.

Cooking tonight?

Don't forget the pickle. It's kind of a big dill.

My wife asked me to sync her phone, so I tossed it into the ocean. I don't know why she's mad at me.

My son keeps saying, "Cheer up Dad, it could be worse, you could be stuck underground in a hole full of water."

But I know he means well.

I dreamed about drowning in an ocean made of orange soda last night.

When I woke up, I realized it was just a Fanta sea.

I've forgotten all my boomerang jokes, but I'm sure they'll come back to me.

If any of you knows of a really good fish pun, let minnow.

An old lady at the bank asked me if I could help her check her balance.

So, I pushed her over.

What rhymes with orange? No it doesn't.

I would avoid eating sushi if I was you. It's a little fishy.

Wanna hear a joke about paper?
Nevermind, it's tearable.

I just read a book about Stockholm
syndrome. It was pretty bad at first, but by
the end I
liked it.

I knew I
shouldn't have had the sea food.

I'm feeling a little eel.

My wife keeps telling me I need to stop pretending to be butter.

But I'm on a roll now.

I wouldn't buy anything with velcro.

It's a complete rip-off.

A proud new Dad sits down with his own father for a celebratory drink.

His father says, "Son, now you've got a child of your own, I think it's time you had this." And with that, he pulls out a book called, *1001 Dad Jokes*. The new dad says, "Dad, I'm honored," as tears well up in his eyes. His father says, "Hi Honored, I'm Dad."

My wife says she's leaving me because she thinks I'm too obsessed with astronomy.

What planet is she on?

I had a dream last night that I was a muffler.

When I woke up I was exhausted.

After dinner my wife asked me if I could clear the table.

I needed a run up, but I made it.

Daughter: Dogs can't operate MRI machines

Dad: But catscan

My son must have been relieved to have finally been born.

He looked like he was running out of womb in there.

I refused to believe my road worker father was stealing from his job, but when I got home all the signs were there.

Don't you hate it when someone answers their own questions? I do.

Hedgehogs, eh?
Why can't they just share the hedge?

My friend keeps trying to convince me that he's a compulsive liar but I just don't believe him.

I always find it hard to explain puns to kleptomaniacs because they're always taking things literally.

I just wrote a song about tortillas; actually, it's more of a rap.

I had a neck brace fitted years ago. I've never looked back since.

I woke up this morning and forgot which side the sun rises from, but then it dawned on me.

I like to hold hands at the movies... which always seems to startle strangers.

I hate Russian dolls, they're so full of themselves.

What's the quickest way to double your money? Dad: "Fold it in half."

Most people pick their nose, but I was just born with mine.

Kid: There's something in my shoe?

Dad: It's your foot.

Have you heard of the band 1023mb? They haven't got a gig yet!

Kid: I'll call you later.

Dad: Don't call me later, call me Dad.

When my wife told me to stop impersonating a flamingo, I had to put my foot down.

I have the heart of a lion and a lifetime ban from the Melbourne Zoo.

A guy walks into a bar and says "ouch!"

I've predicted the events of 2020. You could say I've got 20/20 vision.

I thought that out of these puns, at least 1 in 10 would make me laugh. But no pun in 10 did.

A man tried to sell me a coffin today... I told him that's the last thing I need.

I burned my Hawaiian pizza last night... I should've put it on aloha setting.

I'm terrified of escalators. From now on, I'll be taking steps to avoid them.

Last night me and the wife watched three DVDs back to back. Luckily, I was the one facing the TV.

I'm reading a book on the history of glue. I can't put it down.

RIP boiling water. You shall be mist.

Dad, the man next door has stolen our
garden gate!' –
'Well, don't say
anything in case he
takes offence.

Did you know that
the capital of Ireland is the fastest growing
city in Europe?

It's Dublin every year.

Did you hear about the cartoonist found dead at his home?

Details are
sketchy

I slept like a log
last night.

Woke up in the fireplace!

I went to a seafood disco last week! Pulled a mussel!

I fear for the calendar. It's days are numbered.

I gave away all my used batteries today. Free of charge!

I remember the first time I saw a universal remote control. I thought to myself 'well this changes everything'.

Kid: Apparently, England doesn't have a kidney bank.

Dad: But it does have a Liverpool.

Time flies like an arrow. Fruit flies like a banana.

I don't trust stairs because they're always up to something.

I wasn't going to get a brain transplant. But then I changed my mind.

My cat was just sick on the carpet. I don't think he's
feline well.

Without geometry life is pointless.

People are making apocalypse jokes like there is no tomorrow!

I'd tell you a chemistry joke but I know I wouldn't get a reaction.

Kid: Can I watch TV?

Dad: Yes but don't turn it on.

Kid: Dad, what's the advantage of living in Switzerland?

Dad: Well, the flag is a big plus!

A red and blue ship have collided in the Caribbean Sea. Apparently, the survivors are marooned.

A steak pun is a rare medium well done.

Kid: Dad, can you put my shoes on?

Dad: No, I don't think they'll fit me.

Did you hear about the guy who invented Lifesavers?

They say
he made a
mint.

The only thing worse than having diarrhea is having to spell it.

I keep trying to lose weight, but it keeps finding me.

I don't play soccer because I enjoy the sport. I'm just doing it for kicks.

I went to buy some camouflage trousers the other day, but I couldn't find any.

An invisible man married an invisible woman. The kids were nothing to look at either.

A termite walks into a bar and asks, "Is the bar tender here?"

I needed a password eight characters long so I picked Snow White and the Seven Dwarfs.

Bicycles can't stand on their own, they're two tired.

Kid: "Dad, I've broken my arm in several places."

Dad: "Well don't go to those places."

I'm on a whiskey diet. I've lost three days already.

Atheism is a non-prophet organization.

What's the difference between an African elephant and an Indian elephant?

About 5000 miles

Phone rings

Dad: "If it's for me don't answer it."

I asked my dad for his best dad joke and he said, "You".

I ate a clock yesterday. It was so time consuming.

Egyptians claimed to invent the guitar, but they were such lyres.

I'm thinking about getting a new haircut...

I'm going to
mullet over.

Did you read
about the guy who got killed falling into a
machine at the glasses factory?

Really made a spectacle of himself.

If you want a job in the moisturizer
industry, the best advice I can give is to
apply daily.

I hate perforated lines, they're tearable.

So I came home from work yesterday to find that someone broke into my apartment. Looking around, it seemed like they didn't really take a whole lot. My TV was still there, my PS4, and my Legos were fine. But the apartment was dark, even  when I tried to turn on the lights. Seems the only thing that was taken were my lightbulbs and a couple lamps...I was delighted.

Want to hear a joke about construction? Nah, I'm still working on it.

Son: Where are my sunglasses?

Dad: I don't know...where are my dad glasses?

I have kleptomania. Sometimes when it gets really bad, I take something for it.

You shouldn't kiss anyone on January 1st because it's only the first date.

Want to hear my pizza joke? Never mind, it's too cheesy.

Want to hear a word I just made up? Plagiarism.

My wife is on a tropical food diet, the house is full of the stuff. It's enough to make a mango crazy.

My wife told me I was average, I think she's mean.

Just quit my job at Starbucks because day after day it was the same old grind.

Went to the corner shop today... Bought four corners.

Nostalgia isn't what it used to be.

I used to have a job at the calendar factory, but they fired me because I took a couple of days off.

I have a very secure job. There's nobody else who would want it.

Daughter: How do I look, dad?

Dad: With your eyes, sweetheart.

I told my dad that he should embrace his mistakes. He had tears in his eyes. Then he hugged my sister and me.

Son: Am I adopted?

Dad: Not yet. No one seems interested.

How many pears grow on a tree? All of them.

Dad: How do you like fourth grade?

Son: I don't really like it.

Dad: That's a shame. It was the best three years of
my life!

I buy all of my guns from a guy called "T-Rex". He's a small arms dealer.

If I asked you to choose your favorite feature, would you pick your nose?

My dad asked me, "What do you get when you cross a joke and a rhetorical question?" Then he left.

How do locomotives know where they are going? Lots of training.

Did you hear there's a new type of broom out? It's sweeping the nation.

I thought about going on an all-almond diet.

But that's just nuts.

To whoever stole my copy of Microsoft Office, I will find you. You have my Word!

I went to the zoo and saw a baguette in a cage.

The zookeeper said it was bread in captivity!

What's that place in Nevada where all the dentists visit?

Floss Vegas.

This morning, Siri said, "Don't call me Shirley."

I guess I accidentally left my phone in Airplane mode!

Spring is here! I got so excited ....

... I wet my
plants!

When I told
my wife she drew her eyebrows too high,
she seemed surprised!

I tell dad jokes but I have no kids...

I'm a faux pa!

I know a lot of jokes about retired people...

... but none of them work!

If you see a robbery at an Apple Store does that make you...

... an iWitness?!

I used to work in a shoe-recycling shop.

It was sole destroying!

My boss told me to have a good day...

... so I went
home!

I'm so good at
sleeping...

... I can do it with my eyes closed!

I bought some shoes
from a drug dealer. I
don't know what he
laced them with, but
I was tripping all day!

A three-legged dog walks into a bar and says to the bartender, "I'm looking for the man who shot my paw."

I'm only familiar with 25 letters in the English language. I don't know why.

Waitress: Soup or salad?

Dad: I don't want a SUPER salad, I want a regular salad.

Nurse: Blood type?

Dad: Red.

I was interrogated over the theft of a cheese toastie. Man, they really grilled me.

A computer once beat me at chess, but it was no match for me at kick boxing.

A day without sunshine is like, night.

When tempted to fight fire with fire, remember that fire departments usually use water.

I never start something that I am not going to fi...

Son: Dad, can you give me a hand?

Dad: There's one right there on your arm.

Waiter: How would you like your steak cooked?

Dad: By the chef.

I went to a really emotional wedding the other day. Even the cake was in tiers.

My wife and I were happy for 20 years. But then we met.

Claustrophobic people are more productive thinking outside the box.

I used to be a banker, but over time I lost interest.

The carpenter came around the other day. He made the best entrance I have ever seen...

Telling a demolitionist how to do his job is destructive criticism.

Daughter: Dad, I need to find a job.

Dad: The key to job searching is looking deep within yourself. It's all about the inner view.

A friend of mine tried to annoy me with bird puns, but I soon realized that toucan play at that game.

I tend not to make pig puns. I find them boaring.

I get distracted by all the meats in the deli section, must be my short attention spam.

Son: Dad, my food tastes funny...

Dad: Well, why aren't you laughing?

People who jump off bridges in Paris are in Seine.

I got so angry the other day when I couldn't find my stress ball.

Every night at 11:11, I make a wish that someone will come fix my broken clock.

I can never remember how to spell mnemonic.

Pennies are a dime a dozen.

Daughter: Dad, why are you so late?

Dad: I was listening to some inspirational CDs in the car. They kept telling me to go the extra mile. So I did, and I got lost.

The world tongue-twister champion just got arrested. I hear they're gonna give him a really tough sentence.

Thanks for explaining the word "many" to me, it means a lot.

Son: Is this insecticide good for mosquitos?

Dad: Not at all, it kills them!

Did you hear the joke about the elephant in the elevator? No?

Me neither, I took the stairs.

I used to work for a soft drink can crushing company. It was soda pressing.

When you have a bladder infection, urine trouble.

If life gives you melons, you're probably dyslexic.

You know what they say about paranoid people

My paper towels went missing, so I had to hire a Bounty hunter.

It's not difficult to be an insomniac; I became one overnight.

I don't think women should be allowed to have kids after 40. 40 kids is way too much by any standard.

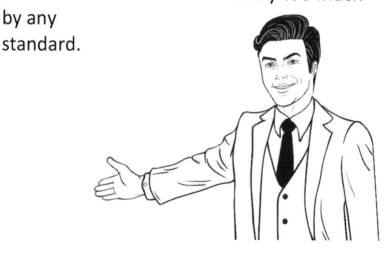

Son: Talk is cheap.

Dad: I guess you've never talked to a lawyer.

My wife's driving test went surprisingly well yesterday. She got 7 out of 12. The other 5 managed to run to safety.

If I got 50 cents for every failed math exam, I'd have $6.30 now.

I had to quit my job at the helium plant. I couldn't tolerate it anymore that people speak to me in such a voice.

I wondered why the frisbee was getting bigger. Then it hit me.

I had a fighting joke. But I forgot the punchline.

Does anyone else find that pressing F5 is refreshing?

Dad: Doctor, I think I have five legs.

Doctor: Oh no!... How do your pants fit?

Dad: Like a glove.

The shovel was a groundbreaking invention.

It's Jamaican hairstyle day at work tomorrow. I'm already dreading it.

It used to cost $2 to change the air pressure in my tires, but now it's $10. That's inflation for you.

Waitress: Here's the check. Can I get you anything else?

Dad: Someone to pay the check?

A farmer in the field with his cows counted 196 of them, but when he rounded them up he had 200.

Daughter: The inventor of the throat lozenge has died.

Dad: I hear there'll be no coffin at his funeral.

Last night I was in bed, gazing up at the stars and thinking... Where's my roof?

Three blondes walk into a bar. You'd think one of them would have seen it.

Son: Do dads always snore?

Dad: Only when we're asleep!

Daughter: Dad, what time is it?

Dad: I don't know, it keeps changing.

I'm selling my broken guitar. No strings attached!

A dry erase board?

That's remarkable!

My wife didn't like my beard... but it grew on me.

Printed in Great Britain
by Amazon